THIS JOURNAL BELONGS TO:

_____
MOM

&

_____
Daughter

Copyright © 2022 by Danielle Fairbairn-Bland

All rights reserved.

No part of this publication may be reproduced, distributed, or transmitted in any form or by any means, including photocopying, recording, or other electronic or mechanical methods, without the prior written permission of the publisher, except in the case of brief quotations embodied in critical reviews and certain other noncommercial uses permitted by copyright law.

Made 2 Heal
New York, NY
ISBN: 978-1-7367094-7-4

For more journals, visit us online at www.deefbland.com or email info@deefbland.com

This book is dedicated to my Mom.
Thank you for being an example of love overflowing.
You instilled values & a foundation that I stand firm on today.

Forever Grateful,
Dee

How to use this book

Journal at your own pace.
There is no right or wrong way to journal. Take your time and figure out what works best for the both of you.

Have an open mind and listen with your heart.
Be open to the experience and listen without judgement.

Make it work for the both of you.
This experience is all about the both of you! Discuss your expectations and what you hope to gain from each other.

Establish rules for privacy.
Discuss the expectations for sharing with others. Can others read the journal? Can you discuss what is shared with others?

Go beyond these pages
This is just the beginning-continue to build and connect outside of these pages.

HAVE FUN!

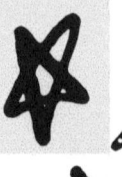

When I first held you in my arms...

Daughter

My first memory of us...

MOM

Having you as my daughter...

# Daughter

Having you as my mom...

Dear MOM,

Love,

I remember when...

Daughter

I remember when...

MOM & Daughter

What does this mean to you both?

JOY

FORGIVENESS

Daughter

You've helped me to...

Watching you grow up, my favorite memory so far is...

 **Daughter**

Growing up, my favorite memory was...

TAKE A MOMENT TO BREATHE.

BREATHE IN...

BREATHE OUT...

BREATHE IN...

BREATHE OUT.

Growing up, my favorite food was...

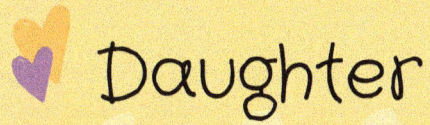 Daughter

Growing up, my favorite food was...

NOTE TO SELF

Dear Daughter,

Love,

OUR MEMORIES

mom

PHOTO HERE

Daughter

PHOTO HERE

OUR RELATIONSHIP
6 words to describe our relationship.

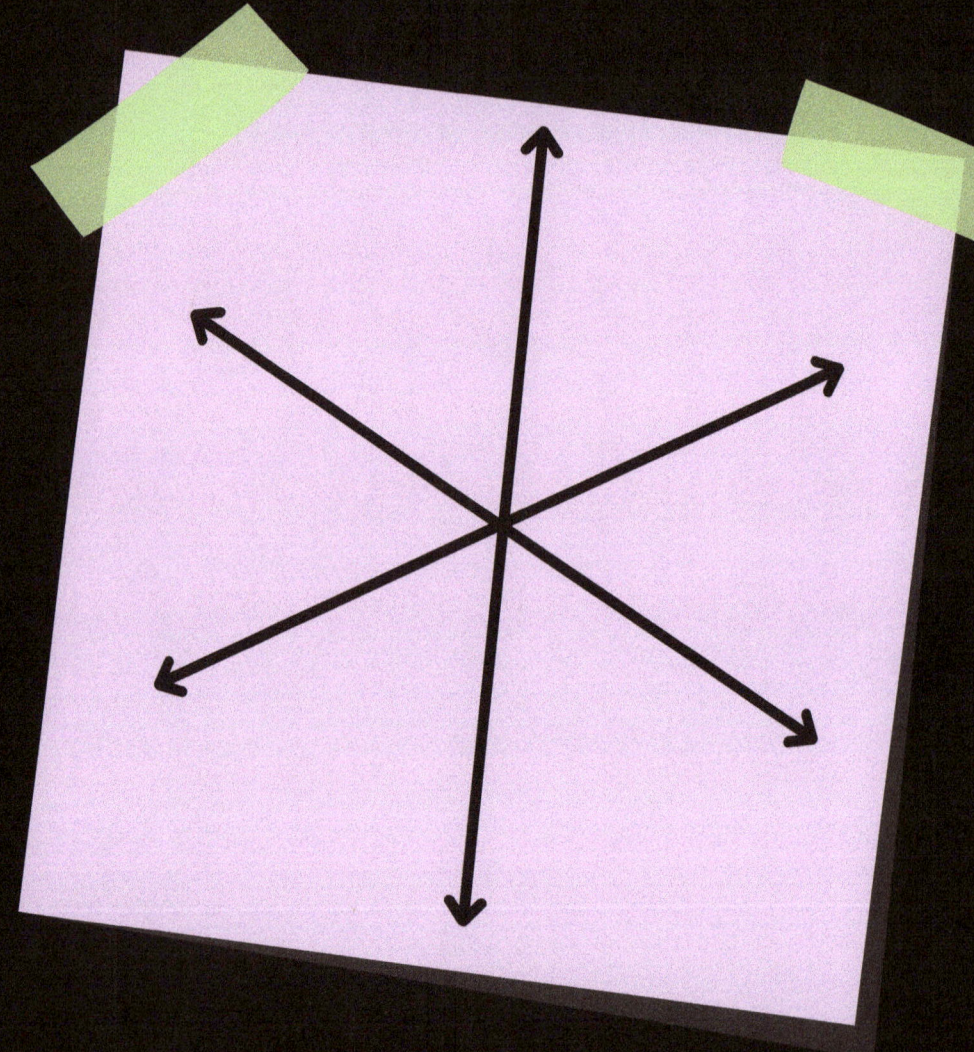

OUR RELATIONSHIP

STRENGTHS OF OUR RELATIONSHIP.

AREAS OF IMPROVEMENT.

OUR RELATIONSHIP

PLACES WE CAN GO TOGETHER.

ACTIVITIES THAT WE CAN DO TOGETHER.

OUR RELATIONSHIP

Here & Now

MOM

When I look at you, I am amazed at how:

Daughter

When I look at you, I am amazed at how:

MOM

If I could travel anywhere right now, I would travel to

Daughter

If I could travel anywhere right now, I would travel to

MOM

MY BUCKET LIST

Daughter

MY BUCKET LIST

MOM

Describe your daughter in 5 words.

Daughter

Describe your mom in 5 words.

I am passionate about...

Daughter

I am passionate about...

The most difficult time in my life...

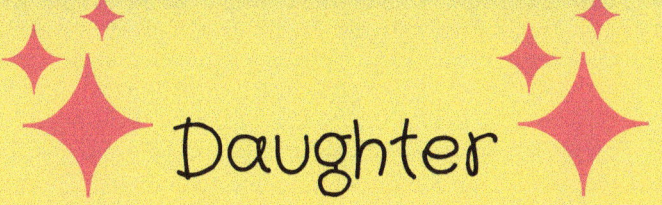

Daughter

The most difficult time in my life...

ASK ME ANYTHING

MOMENT OF GRATITUDE

MOM

DAUGHTER

Dear Daughter,

Love,

Let's talk about Identity
(I can only be ME)

What do you want to share with your daughter?

What do you want to share with your mom?

WHAT DO YOU BOTH WANT TO LEARN MORE ABOUT?

Let's talk about Relationships
(We are better together)

What do you want to share with your daughter?

What do you want to share with your mom?

WHAT DO YOU BOTH WANT TO LEARN MORE ABOUT?

TAKE A MOMENT TO BREATHE.

BREATHE IN...

BREATHE OUT...

BREATHE IN...

BREATHE OUT.

Let's talk about Self Esteem
(Flaws & All)

What do you want to share with your daughter?

What do you want to share with your mom?

WHAT DO YOU BOTH WANT TO LEARN MORE ABOUT?

Let's talk about Personal Development
(Goals | Purpose | Passion)

What do you want to share with your daughter?

What do you want to share with your mom?

WHAT DO YOU BOTH WANT TO LEARN MORE ABOUT?

Let's talk about Finances
(Saving | Investing | Spending | Income)

What do you want to share with your daughter?

What do you want to share with your mom?

WHAT DO YOU BOTH WANT TO LEARN MORE ABOUT?

Let's talk about Health
(Investing in your mind, body and soul)

What do you want to share with your daughter?

What do you want to share with your mom?

WHAT DO YOU BOTH WANT TO LEARN MORE ABOUT?

Let's talk about Mental Wellness
(Inhale, Exhale, Repeat)

What do you want to share with your daughter?

What do you want to share with your mom?

WHAT DO YOU BOTH WANT TO LEARN MORE ABOUT?

Reflections

What did you enjoy about journaling?

What did you learn?

I want to learn more about…

MOM'S
whole heart

www.ingramcontent.com/pod-product-compliance
Lightning Source LLC
Chambersburg PA
CBHW040108120526
44589CB00040B/2824